10/03   26

Maria von Trapp

Maria
von
Trapp

BEYOND

The Sound of Music

CANDICE F. RANSOM

Carolrhoda Books, Inc./Minneapolis

Carolrhoda Books, Inc.
A division of Lerner Publishing Group
241 First Avenue North
Minneapolis, MN 55401 U.S.A.

Website address: www.lernerbooks.com

Library of Congress Cataloging-in-Publication Data

Ransom, Candice F.
    Maria von Trapp: beyond the Sound of Music / by Candice F. Ransom.
        p.   cm.
    ISBN: 1–57505–444–2 (lib. bdg. : alk. paper)
    1. Trapp, Maria Augusta—Juvenile literature. 2. Folk singers—Biography—Juvenile literature. I. Title.
ML3930.T7 R36 2002
782.42'092-dc21   00–011449

Manufactured in the United States of America
1 2 3 4 5 6 – JR – 07 06 05 04 03 02

Contents

Cast of Characters

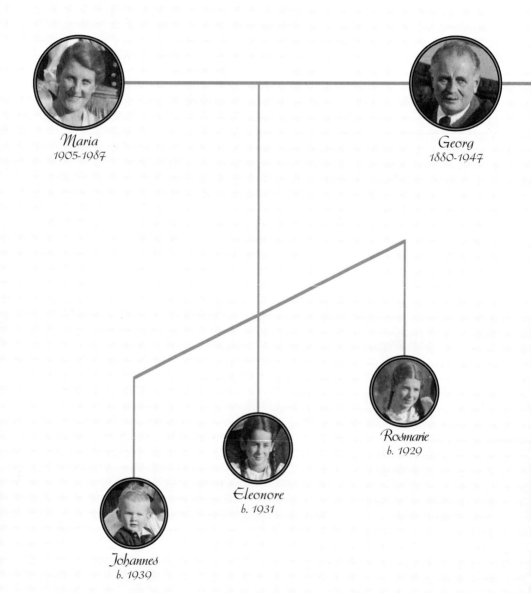

Maria
1905-1987

Georg
1880-1947

Rosmarie
b. 1929

Eleonore
b. 1931

Johannes
b. 1939

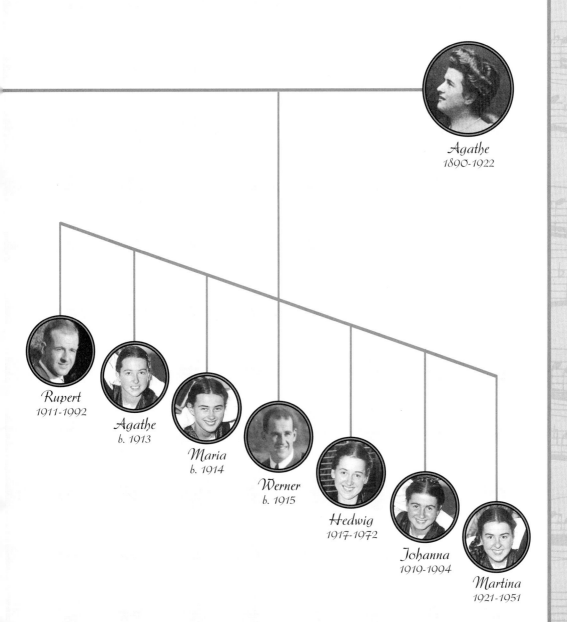

Agathe
1890-1922

Rupert
1911-1992

Agathe
b. 1913

Maria
b. 1914

Werner
b. 1915

Hedwig
1917-1972

Johanna
1919-1994

Martina
1921-1951

Maria described herself as "a very lonesome child."

1

Make-Believe Family

The furniture was arranged in a neat circle. Every stool, chair, and hassock from the parlor and dining room was crowded into the sitting room. Seven-year-old Maria Augusta Kutschera poured tea into a china cup and offered it to her father in the chair next to her. Her blue eyes widened as he told her about the new calf. She clapped a hand to her plump pink cheek when her mother said this would be the best crop ever. And Maria squealed with delight when one of her brothers tugged the bow in her light brown hair.

How she loved her family! She had so much fun being a farmer's daughter, with eleven brothers and sisters to play with.

Suddenly the sitting room door opened. Maria's foster mother eyed the scene with exasperation. Her best chairs were standing in a circle again! But no one sat in them.

Maria waited for her foster mother to scold her. Then she promised not to move the furniture or play pretend family again. As she carried the chairs back, Maria sighed. It wasn't that she didn't love the people she lived with. Her foster mother was usually kind, except when she caught Maria chattering to the invisible Paultraxl family. It was just that everyone in the dim, silent house was so *old*.

Maria lived with her foster mother and foster sister in a small stone farmhouse in the Austrian town of Kagran. Kagran was on the outskirts of Vienna, the capital of Austria and one of the world's great cities. But Maria knew little of the world beyond the tall wooden gates that connected the farmhouses in Kagran. She watched hay wagons pass through those gates. She collected milk and potatoes from the neighboring farmers. And she longed for playmates her own age.

Maria's foster mother was actually her father's elderly cousin. Maria's four foster brothers and sisters were grown up. Only her foster mother's daughter Kathy lived at home, and she was more like an aunt than a sister. Her foster mother didn't like the racket of young children, so Maria couldn't invite her friends home after school. Kathy escorted her to school and picked her up every day. Maria wasn't allowed to visit at other houses either. She couldn't even walk home from school with any of her girlfriends.

Out of loneliness, Maria had invented the noisy, loving Paultraxl family. When her imaginary world was banished from the house, Maria simply transferred it to the garden. There she "baked" sand Viennese cakes to serve at her "parties."

Maria often wondered about her true family. In a way, her real parents seemed as make-believe as the Paultraxls. No one talked much about Maria's mother and father. But over the years, she pieced together a story from conversations she'd overheard.

Her real father, Karl Kutschera, was an engineer from Vienna. As a young man, he had met a girl named Clara. They married and had a son they named Karl. One spring day, Maria's father and Clara drove their buggy across a bridge. The horse shied, tipping the buggy over the rail. Maria's father survived, but Clara drowned. Heartbroken, the young man took his son, Karl, to a trusted cousin. Then he traveled all over the world.

When Maria's father finally came home, he visited Clara's grave. There he saw a beautiful young girl who looked like his dead wife! The girl's name was Augusta. Karl called her Gusti and eventually married her.

Karl and Gusti lived happily together in Vienna. Soon they were expecting a baby. Gusti found city life exciting, but she was also homesick for the craggy, snow-capped Alps of her hometown. Gusti was from the province of Tirol, which means "land in the mountains." And what mountains! Wildspitz and more than seven hundred other peaks were popular places to go climbing and skiing. She visited her family over Christmas,

Maria's parents, Karl and Augusta Kutschera

promising to return to Vienna to have her baby. But on the train ride home, the baby arrived early. Even as a newborn baby, impatient Maria Augusta just couldn't wait! Her baptism certificate stated she was born in a Viennese hospital on January 26, 1905. But Maria knew she was actually born on a train from Tirol on January 25.

Gusti died of pneumonia when Maria was only a toddler, and Maria did not remember her mother at all. Maria's father took her to the same cousin who had raised his older son. The cousin, Maria's foster mother, had been in her sixties, but she welcomed Maria. Once more Maria's father left to wander the world alone.

Since that time, Maria's father had returned home, but he never claimed his daughter. Maria remained with her foster mother and saw her father occasionally. Her father's world was so different from the stone farmhouse where Maria lived. When she visited him at his apartment in Vienna, her curious blue eyes would sweep over rooms filled with books and strange musical instruments. Most fascinating of all was the aviary. Maria's father had covered the doorway of one room with netting. Inside, tiny birds flitted like scraps of colored paper, trilling happy songs.

Maria was in awe of this older man, who could speak fourteen languages and play those forbidding-looking instruments. She felt uncomfortable around him. He didn't talk with her but at her. If she showed an interest in the bass cello, he would play it for her. Then he expected her to play it as well. Maria could make plinking or tootling sounds, nothing like the beautiful music her father played. If she touched one of his books, her father would read a passage in Turkish or Latin. Young Maria shrank when he asked her to repeat the foreign words.

Maria stands awkwardly next to her father.

When her father gave her a diary, she faithfully recorded daily events. Maria knew her father had kept journals all his life. But she didn't know what to write on her own blank pages. *I got up at seven o'clock. I had to do my own hair. Had eggs for breakfast . . . .* How dull!

Worst of all were the educational trips. Her father insisted that Maria become more worldly. But she didn't want to leave Vienna. She didn't care about the beauty of the Danube River or the majestic glaciers of Austria. Homesick, she cried until her angry father took her home. Maria felt like a disappointment. No wonder her father didn't want her.

When Maria was nine, her life changed dramatically. That year her father died. She had no more chances to prove she was a worthy daughter.

Uncle Franz became Maria's guardian. He was a judge, married to her foster mother's daughter, Anni. They had moved into the stone house with Maria's foster mother. Maria had always known Uncle Franz as a stern man. For Maria, he became a monster.

Maria was in her fifth year, the last year of grammar school. Kathy had stopped accompanying her to and from school. Usually Maria walked with her girlfriends. Overnight, she could no longer hang around her friends. Her uncle tolerated no foolishness. Maria was instructed to come straight home from school. There would be no more talking to her friends or dawdling to look in the shops. Even when she practically ran home after class, her uncle would be waiting in the doorway with a stick. Insisting she had been up to no good, he spanked her.

Uncle Franz punished her for imagined crimes: spending her school supply money on candy, skipping school, playing with girlfriends. Maria could do nothing right, and she lived in fear of her uncle. Her foster mother and Anni sobbed behind closed doors. Like so many families in the early 1900s, when the man of the house laid down the law, the women were expected to obey. The judge was a man who stood for no arguments. But by the time Maria was thirteen, she had decided she didn't want to live in fear any longer. She suddenly realized she might as well commit those crimes. She was going to be punished anyway!

Until then, Maria had always been a shy and quiet girl. She had been raised around adults with their set ways. And she had grown up in an isolated, rural part of town. No one had ever encouraged Maria to express herself—not her foster mother, not her father, and certainly not her uncle. Maria's locked-away spirit burst forth like a lion from a cage.

She became outspoken and boisterous at school. She laughed loudly during lessons, made jokes, and entertained the other girls with her antics. Maria was the class cutup. She would do anything for attention. And instead of heading home after school, Maria visited her friends and stayed as long as she liked. When Uncle Franz spanked her, she didn't care. At least she'd had fun!

In high school, Maria played hooky, hiking the meadows around Kagran alone. She came back home with bunches of wildflowers, which she put in vases and jars around the house. The flowers were proof of her defiant acts.

Though she acted up in and out of class, Maria still managed to get good grades. But her report cards showed that her conduct was unacceptable. Maria had gone from being an ideal student to every teacher's worst nightmare.

At fifteen, Maria was finishing her last year of high school. Her reign as teacher's terror was nearly over. Yet she was still a willful, untamed girl. What would her life bring?

2

The Tomboy Nun

Although Maria had given her teachers a rough time, she aspired to become a teacher herself. After graduating from high school, she applied to the State Teachers' College of Progressive Education.

Uncle Franz sneered at her. Where would she get the money? he asked her. If Maria had been older, she would have demanded an accounting of her father's estate. What had happened to his money? Or the collections of books and musical instruments? But Maria never thought to question her financial position. She had been dependent on relatives all her life, but somehow she was going to take charge of her own life. She didn't need a family.

Maria was a determined young woman. This picture was taken when Maria was a teenager.

A classmate also shared Maria's dream of attending teachers' college. Annie was used to making her own way. She told Maria she often earned money in her home town, which was a summer resort. Annie urged Maria to stay with her family and work at the resort, saving her wages for tuition.

Maria knew this was her one chance to escape. Three days after graduation, she secretly packed her nightgown, toothbrush, some books, and a couple of dresses in a huge straw suitcase. When Uncle Franz took his daily nap, she crept into his room and stole his pocket change. Kissing her foster mother and Kathy good-bye, she ran to catch the next trolley. At the train station, she purchased a one-way ticket to Semmering, Annie's hometown.

When Maria arrived in Semmering, she walked to Annie's house. Although there were seven children in Annie's family, Annie's mother generously let Maria live with them. Maria had to sleep on the floor, but she was excited. At last, she was in control of her destiny.

The day after she arrived, Maria trudged from hotel to hotel, seeking a teaching job. Surely there were wealthy guests whose children needed tutoring during the summer. But she looked like a child herself, rail thin, her hair in two braids that brushed her kneecaps. No one would take her seriously.

When that didn't work, Maria made the rounds again, pleading for any kind of job. A hotel manager asked if she could umpire a tennis tournament. Maria had never heard the term *umpire* before, much less played tennis, but she gamely agreed. For the next week, she sat on a high stool on the tennis court and called the plays.

On the last day of the tournament, Maria looked down and saw Uncle Franz. Her heart hammered. He had followed her! Finding courage she didn't know she possessed, she whispered to him to leave immediately, or she would yell. Her uncle said he wanted to make sure she was all right. Maria nodded, and he left. She never saw him again. Years later when he was committed to an insane asylum, Maria realized he had been a sick man.

Maria worked at the hotel the rest of the summer. In September, she and Annie had saved enough money to enroll in the state teachers' college in Vienna. Because

Vienna around 1920

Maria was an orphan, she received a scholarship. The scholarship paid for tuition, room, and board. Maria had to earn money for clothes, textbooks, and supplies. On Saturdays, she went to the Imperial Palace in Vienna to pick up embroidery work. For embroidering slips and pillowcases, she was paid by the inch.

Maria was busy with school and work, but she still found time for fun. Though she had no money for concerts, one of her favorite forms of entertainment was music. The songbirds in the meadows around Kagran had opened up Maria's ears to music. And despite her unpleasant music lessons with her father, she had been enchanted by his musical talents.

Luckily for Maria, Vienna was famous for opera and classical music. On any given day, there was a variety of musical events, some of them free. Cathedrals and churches were another source of free music. They were always sponsoring programs. Maria could hear the Vienna Philharmonic or listen to the Vienna Boys' Choir. She ignored the sermons. She only went to church for the music.

Maria had tussled with religion most of her life. When she was a little girl, she had obediently attended Mass with her foster mother. She'd enjoyed Bible stories and prayed faithfully. But when Uncle Franz became her guardian, she changed. Her uncle was a socialist. He believed that the government should control school and

Performances at places such as the Vienna Opera House were common when Maria lived there. The city made her "hungry for music."

work for the good of everyone. Like other socialists, he had no use for the church. Living under his roof, Maria cut religion out of her life.

Maria couldn't avoid religion entirely. Although the state teachers' college prided itself on being a modern school, religion was still a required class. Many of the girls gave the theology professor a hard time. Maria was the worst of all. Scornful of the Catholic girls in her class, Maria was determined to "beat" the "holy water girls," as she called them. She and a group of students strived for higher grades than the religious girls, without going to confession or counting beads on a rosary.

Four years of college passed quickly for Maria. During her last year, she walked into a church on Palm Sunday, expecting to hear music. Instead there was a sermon. The church was so crowded, Maria couldn't leave. When the program was over, she boldly asked the Jesuit priest if he really believed what he had preached. The priest asked Maria if she would like to talk further. He made an appointment with her for the following Tuesday. Maria didn't want to go, but she hated the idea of the priest thinking she was a coward.

At that meeting, Maria aired her doubts. Then she listened to the priest. When the sun streaming through the window appeared to give the priest a halo, she suddenly experienced a strange lightness. Maria was so enchanted, she didn't remember walking outside. On the street, she stumbled into a trolley car. She wasn't hurt, but she wasn't the same, either. That talk with the priest had changed her somehow.

A week of hiking in the majestic Alps changed Maria's life forever.

After graduation, Maria and her classmates hiked the Alps for a week. Throughout her school years, she and her friends often strolled through the Vienna woods, and in the summer, they hiked all over Austria. One day during the hike, Maria was the last to reach a cliff. The sunset bathed the snowbanks in pink and tangerine hues. On top of the glacier, Maria flung her arms wide and asked God what he wanted from her.

She decided that she should give up everything she enjoyed in the world and devote her life to God. No more hiking or mountain climbing or having fun with her friends. She would join a convent. And she would start *that moment.*

Impulsive as always, nineteen-year-old Maria said good-bye to her friends, walked down the mountain, and caught a train to Salzburg, the nearest city. When she arrived in Salzburg the next morning, she asked a police officer which convent was the strictest. If she was going to give up her life, she would not do it halfway. She learned that the Benedictine abbey of Nonnberg was the harshest convent. Still wearing her hiking outfit, with a coil of rope over her shoulder and an icepick in her hand, Maria climbed the 144 steps up the mountain to the eighth-century abbey.

Impatiently ringing the bell, Maria asked to see "the boss." She was shown into a room and was greeted by the Reverend Mother Abbess. The Reverend Mother asked Maria why she had come to the convent.

Holding her icepick in a grand gesture, Maria announced, "I have come to stay!"

The Reverend Mother then inquired who had sent her to them.

"Ha!" Maria declared. "If anybody had sent me, I wouldn't be here! I haven't obeyed anybody yet."

Despite her outburst, or perhaps because of it, Maria was admitted into the abbey. She became a postulant, which is the stage one must pass through before becoming a novice. The stages were necessary in a nun's education. It was one thing to say one wanted to devote one's life to serving God. Living in a convent and abiding by its rules tested a candidate's true faith.

As a postulant, Maria was given a black dress and a black mantilla, a scarf that covered her long, light hair.

Her regular clothes were donated to charity. But it would take more than a demure outfit to turn Maria into a nun. She became the first tomboy in the Holy Order of Saint Benedict. She also became the first candidate for the novitiate to be assigned her own private Mistress of Novices. Looking after Maria became a full-time job!

It was never hard to tell where Maria was. Her footsteps clattered over the cobblestoned floors. The ancient walls echoed her bubbling laughter. The crash of china often shattered the holy quiet. Maria didn't mean to be a trial, but she just couldn't help herself. So many things were forbidden. Why couldn't she whistle in the halls? What was wrong with taking the steps two at a time? Sliding down the spiral banister was much quicker than mincing down the stairs.

After years of freely roaming the countryside, it was difficult to be cooped up in a cloister. Maria missed the meadows and mountains, which could be glimpsed from the room she shared with three other candidates. She tried to be good, but she was continually being punished for her boisterous ways. Her morning prayers grew longer, as she vowed not to climb on the roof and jump over the chimney or not to tickle another novice and make her laugh during deep silence.

Maria also had to adjust to a strict routine at the abbey. She rose at five in the morning, dressed, prayed an hour and a half in Latin, attended daily Mass, ate breakfast, and performed her assigned chores—all in complete silence. A one o'clock bell signaled the end of silence for a single hour.

By this time, Maria was exploding with questions and comments. But the other postulants wanted to talk, too. Sometimes the entire hour raced by without Maria being able to say a word. At two o'clock sharp, the bell rang again and silence once more fell over the abbey.

Despite the strict routine and many rules, Maria thrived in the abbey. For the first time in her life, she felt secure. Nonnberg was beginning to feel like the loving home she'd never had.

Nonnberg Abbey

In September, Maria was assigned to teach a class of fifth graders at a school run by the abbey. She adored her children and was a very popular teacher. Her college education flew out the window. Instead of launching into a dusty lesson, Maria would start the day with a song. She had learned to play the guitar and enjoyed leading sing-alongs. Between September and Christmas, her class learned forty-seven songs and heard numerous stories. Then Maria realized that she had forgotten to teach any arithmetic or grammar! She confessed to her students that they would have to work hard to make up for lost time. Luckily, her students were good sports, and soon they were caught up in their schooling.

That first year passed quickly into another. During Maria's time at the abbey, the nuns had become her large, loving family, and Maria thought of her students as her own children. She sat on the floor with them, sang with them, and got her hands dirty with modeling clay. The superintendent of schools praised Maria's teaching methods.

Maria had only to obtain her Master of Education degree. Then she would enter the convent as a novice. The heavy oak doors would shut away the outside world forever.

Maria was ready.

3

Maria on Loan

Maria's heart thudded as she left her classroom, where she had been grading papers. The Reverend Mother Abbess never sent for a lowly candidate.

As Maria climbed the spiral stairway to the abbess's private quarters, she wondered what she had done wrong. Twenty-one-year-old Maria had grown up a lot at the abbey. Her behavior had improved since her tomboy days, but she still got into trouble from time to time. And she still had to pass the final test in order to become a novice. Was the Reverend Mother displeased with her? Her knees felt weak as she knocked on the Reverend Mother's solid oak door.

The Reverend Mother greeted Maria, then asked her what she had learned during her stay at Nonnberg. Maria was relieved. She immediately replied, "The most important thing in life is to find out what is the will of God and then to go and do it."

The abbess seemed pleased with Maria's answer. Then she spoke of a Captain von Trapp who had come seeking a governess for one of his seven motherless children. Young Maria von Trapp was recovering from scarlet fever and could not go to school. It was the will of God, the Reverend Mother concluded firmly, that Maria leave the abbey and go teach the little girl.

Maria was stunned. Leave her home? The ancient gray stone walls made her feel secure. The quiet routine was comforting. At Nonnberg, Maria felt safe. She felt loved. And now she would have to go outside the cloister walls.

Only for nine months, the Reverend Mother assured her.

Maria still didn't like the idea. She would be on loan, like a library book, to a sea captain, yet. Captain von Trapp was probably a gruff old man. His house would be filled with lion skins and native spears, collected on his travels.

But there was no arguing with the Reverend Mother's decision. It was October 1926. Maria would be able to return to the abbey the following June. With that consoling thought, she prepared for her journey into the outside world.

When postulants entered the abbey, they gave their clothing to the poor. Only the most recent candidate's clothes were available, in case someone had to leave. Maria wished the last postulant had been a bit more fashionable. The blue serge dress was too big for Maria's slender figure. Heavy black stockings and clumpy black shoes made her look even dowdier. Topping off the outfit was an ugly leather hat that came down over her ears like a fireman's helmet.

With her guitar and satchel of books, Maria sadly descended the 144 steps into Salzburg. She caught a bus to Aigen, a village twenty minutes outside the city, and obtained directions to the Von Trapp villa.

When she saw the stone mansion, Maria stopped in amazement. An ivy-covered tower rose imposingly into the sky. Tall horse chestnut trees shaded the wide lawn. An endless wrought-iron fence surrounded the estate. Maria walked through the gate and up to the double arched oak doors. Nervously, she rang the bell. The door was opened by a gentleman wearing white gloves.

Maria held out her hand and said, "How do you do, Captain?"

The large Von Trapp villa in winter

This photograph of the Von Trapp children was probably taken before Maria arrived. Pictured (from LEFT TO RIGHT) are Martina, Johanna, Hedwig, Werner, Maria, Agathe, and Rupert.

The man bowed stiffly and introduced himself as Hans, the butler. Then he ushered Maria into the great hall.

To Maria's surprise, there were no lion skins or native spears. An enormous Austrian flag draped one wall. When she met the captain himself, her image of the gruff old seaman instantly vanished. Captain von Trapp was neither old nor crusty. He was a broad-shouldered, distinguished-looking gentleman with brown hair and an impressive mustache.

When the captain blew a brass whistle shrilly, Maria was startled. Then, to her amazement, four girls and two boys in blue sailor suits marched down the stairs. The children lined up for Maria to inspect. Fifteen-year-old Rupert was the oldest. The youngest was Martina, age six. In between were fourteen-year-old Agathe, eleven-year-old Werner, ten-year-old Hedwig, and eight-year old Johanna. The child Maria had come to care for, thirteen-year-old Maria, was the only one not present. She was in bed, recovering from her illness.

Six pairs of dark eyes stared at Maria. Six pale, serious faces studied her. In order to see them better, Maria pushed back the ugly hat, which tumbled at Johanna's feet. The little girl giggled.

The captain next took Maria upstairs to meet young Maria. The little girl lay against piled pillows. She spoke politely to her new teacher. On their way back down-stairs, the captain explained that his wife had died four years earlier. Maria was the twenty-sixth in a long line of teachers and governesses.

Twenty-six teachers in four years! Maria thought.

Maria was then shown to her room. The antique bed was draped in pale blue silk. A chandelier sparkled over a plush oriental rug. After living in the sparsely deco-rated abbey, Maria was not accustomed to such lavish surroundings. She felt homesick.

Nine months, Maria told herself. Surely she could en-dure anything for nine months.

The Von Trapp estate was run by a housekeeper. She informed Maria that the captain was a retired naval hero. He was also a baron. Maria learned the story of the baron and his first wife over pastries in the housekeeper's ruffle-filled room. After the baroness's death, the captain hired many nurses and teachers. He loved his children, the housekeeper gossiped, but was shy with them.

Georg and Agathe von Trapp. Before Agathe died of scarlet fever in 1922, she asked Georg to remarry so that their children would be cared for.

Maria worried about her new charge, who was completely housebound. Maria von Trapp was dutiful and sickly. So when the little girl wistfully remarked she missed playing the piano, Maria had one of the violins in the music room brought to her. Then Maria hired a woman to give young Maria lessons. The child was a natural musician, so different from Maria, who had made horrible tweetles on her father's instruments!

Maria knew she was responsible for young Maria only, but it turned out that all of the children needed her. The younger children longed for attention, and the older children were too careful and quiet. Despite the lovely gardens and parkland, the children never played outside. They only took "healthful" walks. Children should be rowdy and allowed to run about, Maria believed, not kept on a shelf like art objects. She herself had grown up among adults who did not like children making noise. She firmly believed that children should laugh and play freely!

Maria tried to make changes. She asked the housekeeper to buy hooded woolen capes for the children for rainy weather. The housekeeper replied that the captain wanted his children to carry umbrellas, even though the children lost them. And there was no way the children could play in that wonderful backyard wearing white sailor outfits. Eventually Maria convinced the housekeeper to buy playsuits, sandals, and a volleyball net. Soon the children were playing sports outdoors.

But Maria did more than play games with the Von Trapp children. On school mornings, she woke them, saw to their breakfasts, and sent the older ones to school. Besides tutoring young Maria during the day, she taught Johanna and befriended shy Martina. When Johanna climbed into her lap and kissed her one day, Maria responded with a hug. Her own foster mother had been kind but never hugged or kissed Maria. And Uncle Franz was hardly someone Maria could throw her arms around. The baron's children were hungry for affection. And so was Maria.

One rainy November Saturday, Rupert, Agathe, young Maria, and Werner came to the nursery, where Maria was playing with the younger children. The older children weren't supposed to be there. The housekeeper wanted the older boys in their room, the girls in theirs. Only at mealtimes were the children together. Maria thought the rule was silly and chose to ignore it this morning. She liked the feeling of having the whole large family together.

Werner saw Maria's guitar, and he wondered if she could play it. Maria picked it up. Eagerly, the children gathered around. What song did they want to hear? she asked them. They didn't know any songs. Maria was flabbergasted. They didn't know *any* songs?

Maria suggested a few. The children shook their heads. They only knew some navy songs from their father. And they knew "Silent Night." Maria taught them some songs and encouraged them to sing three-part harmony, each taking a different part. The children had fine voices. Maria taught them some folk songs. They were having a wonderful time when the housekeeper put an end to the songfest. The baron, she said, forbade the girls to sit on the floor.

Maria refused to let the baron's rules discourage her. One evening during another songfest, the baron walked in unexpectedly. Maria was afraid the captain would be upset when he saw the children all together in the nursery and the girls sitting on the floor. To her surprise, he was delighted to discover his musical family. Immediately he settled on the floor surrounded by the children, with Martina and Johanna on his knees. He picked up the violin and played for them. The baron praised the children's voices over and over. After the singing, he asked them about school and what they had been working on lately.

Maria watched the tender scene, realizing the distant baron was an image created by the housekeeper. In reality, he was affectionate around his children. It was obvious the children loved him as well.

By Christmas, Maria was very much a part of the family. She ordered that decorations be hung in the nursery, not in the cold reception room downstairs. The children's room had become the heart of the Von Trapp villa. On Christmas Eve, the huge tree was set up in the nursery.

The baron began spending more time with his children. He often joined Maria and the children in games. As winter thawed into spring, they went bicycling and hiking.

That spring, Maria learned of Princess Yvonne, a distant cousin of the baron's wife, who was coming for a visit. The housekeeper said the baron wanted to remarry, and she hinted that Princess Yvonne and the baron would probably become engaged. Maria pictured a beautiful fairy-tale princess, sweet-natured and eager to be a mother. She was glad. The children would have a mother again. But the children weren't happy. They told Maria their father didn't need to marry anyone now that Maria had come.

The princess arrived the next day. She greeted Maria coolly, calling her the "wonder girl" she'd heard about. Later, when the two of them were alone, the princess announced that the baron was in love with Maria. Maria was stunned. How could this be? She was only the children's teacher!

Yvonne reassured Maria that she still planned to marry the baron. Maria would give the children a little party on the wedding day, since they would not be attending the ceremony. After the honeymoon, the children would be sent away to boarding school. Then Maria could return to the abbey, her duties completed.

*The dashing Georg von Trapp
in his naval uniform*

Maria's thoughts were in a turmoil. She respected the baron and was fond of him, but it was the children she loved. She couldn't believe the baron was in love with *her*. And what would become of the children? Princess Yvonne would not be a good mother. How could the children be happy in boarding schools?

It was clear the children wanted Maria to stay, but she had not abandoned her goal of becoming a nun. And she had become uncomfortable around the baron. If he offered to open a door, she stiffly said she could do it herself. The baron seemed confused by her behavior. He didn't seem to know what Princess Yvonne had told Maria.

In May, the baron went to see Princess Yvonne. Thinking he would become engaged, Maria agreed to stay until the end of June, as promised. Then she would return to the convent. But the baron came home early. For days, he locked himself in his study. Maria was worried. It was only two weeks until the end of June. If the baron was engaged, he didn't fit her idea of a happy man.

One morning when Maria was spring cleaning, Martina, Johanna, and Hedwig knocked on the baron's study door. Maria was balanced on a ladder washing the crystals of the chandelier when the little girls came out again.

"Father says he doesn't know whether you like him or not at all!" they said.

"Why, of course I like him," Maria murmured, intent upon her task.

That evening as Maria arranged flowers, the baron came over to her. He asked her why she hadn't told him she had accepted his proposal of marriage.

Maria dropped the scissors. Peony petals fell to the floor. *What* had he said?

Apparently the children had informed their father that the only way to keep her in the family was for him to marry her. The baron told them he'd love to marry Maria, but he didn't think she liked him enough to marry him. Maria suddenly remembered the little girls asking her if she liked their father that morning.

"But Captain," she said now, "you know that in a very short while I shall go back to my convent; and one cannot enter a convent and marry at the same time."

The baron looked sad. "Is this your very last word? Is there absolutely no hope?"

Confused, Maria fled to the abbey. She poured her heart out to the Reverend Mother. But she did not feel comforted by the Reverend Mother's words. The abbess told her gently that it was the will of God that she marry the baron. Maria was deeply disappointed. She had planned to devote her life to God and now she was rejected. Once more, it was as if she did not measure up. Her father had made her feel that way. And nothing she ever did pleased Uncle Franz. The door of the abbey was closed forever to her, too.

With a heavy heart, Maria returned to the villa. The baron was waiting for her.

4

A Most Unusual Family

The bells of Nonnberg tolled, their rich tones ringing over the valley. Maria bowed her head as her Mistress of Novices placed the circlet of edelweiss blossoms on her wedding veil. It was time to go. Maria knelt to receive the blessing from the Reverend Mother.

As she entered the church, Maria saw that the entire town had packed the pews. Agathe and Hedwig led the baron to the altar. He stood handsome and tall in his naval uniform. The three youngest girls straightened the train of Maria's gown. The organ began to play. Slowly Maria walked up the steps. It was November 26, 1927. Twenty-two-year-old Maria had started this day as an awkward girl. She ended the day as the new Baroness von Trapp, wife of Georg, and mother of seven children.

Adjusting to her new life wasn't easy. Instead of becoming the bride of Christ, as she had planned, she was given to this man! Hadn't she always followed the will of God? Why did he lead her to this marriage? The will of

On her wedding day, Maria was still "blazing mad" about having to marry Georg.

God and the will of Maria clashed. She was angry at both God and her husband. Before leaving on her honeymoon, Maria urged Georg to go without her because Werner had a fever. Georg simply postponed the trip.

As mistress of the villa, Maria had domestic matters to attend to. The servants looked to her for their instructions. Maria had never paid attention to how houses were run. In the abbey, everything had been done for her. Remembering that the first baroness had kept tight reins on the household, Maria reluctantly went into the staff's quarters to issue the next day's orders. She wanted to tell them to do as they pleased, but she realized very little work would get done with that attitude.

As Christmas approached, Maria made excuses not to go to church. But she attended midnight Mass on Christmas Eve so the children wouldn't be disappointed. In the parish church, Maria listened to the moving story of the birth of Christ. She heard sweet carols sung. Her bitterness dissolved and she let God and her husband into her heart. Christmas Day, not November 26, became the day Maria and Georg celebrated their wedding anniversary.

At last Maria had everything she had longed for—a houseful of children, a loving husband, and her faith. Maria spent her days running the Von Trapp household, with little Martina trailing after her. In the evenings after supper, the whole family gathered before a crackling fire. Maria read stories aloud. Then they would sing together. On weekends they hiked and cycled.

For Maria, life was perfect. But she was keenly aware of the fact she was the second wife, and that Georg's first marriage had been very happy. How could she make her husband that happy once more? As always, whenever Maria made up her mind to do something, she threw her soul into it. She asked Georg how she could make him happiest. He replied she should be just like his first wife.

Maria visited relatives to find out what the baron's first wife was like. The first Baroness von Trapp was quiet. She detested sports and hiking. She liked to knit. So Maria gave up hiking and playing volleyball. A nun taught her to knit. In the evenings, she sat demurely knitting, just like Georg's first wife. Georg wanted to know why she didn't go bicycling anymore. Why didn't they sing together? And *why* was she knitting that awful stocking?

Tearfully Maria explained. Georg tossed the knitting in the corner. Then he said he meant that Maria should be as kind as his first wife. More important, he wanted Maria to be herself. *That* Maria could do. Once more the Von Trapp family took up hiking and singing. And the family grew. In 1929, Maria gave birth to Rosmarie, whom they affectionately called Illi. Two years later, Eleonore, nicknamed Lorli, was born.

Although her large, loving family climbed mountains together and sang folk songs by the hour on long summer evenings, Maria knew the rest of the world was not as content. A shadow loomed over Europe. Austrian-born Adolf Hitler became Germany's dictator in 1933. His power seemed boundless. Georg predicted terrible times ahead. After returning from vacation one September, Georg learned the bank that handled the Von Trapp investments was ruined. Hitler had closed the Austrian border to Germans. Austria was a small country, dependent on tourism. Many banks and businesses failed as a result.

While most of their money was lost, the Von Trapps had enough to pay bills. They also had the villa and many paintings and art objects. But their lifestyle would have to change. Georg sold the car and let most of the staff go, keeping only the butler and cook. The first and second floors of the mansion were closed off. The family lived on the third floor. The children pitched in to help with gardening and household chores. Georg was upset

Father Franz Wasner became an important member of the Von Trapp family.

by their financial state, but Maria took it in stride. Not even bankruptcy could dampen her spirits.

"Aren't we lucky, Georg, that we lost that money," she said. "How would we ever have found out what fine fellows the children are?" Maria showed him they didn't need money and servants. They still had each other. And they were their own best resource.

Soon Maria realized their spacious mansion could be put to use. Why not open the house to students from the nearby seminary? At first Georg balked at turning his baronial estate into a rooming house. Then he relented. Maria had a way of making him see things differently. It wasn't shameful to be without money—it was an adventure.

Everyone cleaned the closed off rooms, changed the bed linens and became innkeepers. Within a year, the Von Trapp villa was filled with boarders. One of their theological visitors was thirty-four-year-old Father Wasner.

The round-faced young priest came to the villa to say Mass one Sunday in the spring of 1935. A teacher of Gregorian chant at the seminary, he was impressed by the Von Trapp family's musical abilities. At the breakfast table that morning, Father Wasner conducted Maria and the children through a verse. Though he appreciated their unpolished voices, he suggested ways to improve their style.

Father Wasner began to rehearse Maria and the children nearly every day. His boundless enthusiasm made four- and five-hour rehearsals fly by. Simple folk tunes gave way to serious motets and masses. Under his direction, the Von Trapps progressed from four-part harmony to polyphonic music—music with more than one melody. They

A music rehearsal at the Von Trapp villa. Pictured (from LEFT TO RIGHT) are: Young Maria, Martina, Agathe, Rupert, Maria, Johanna, Hedwig, and Werner.

learned everything by heart, their rich, varied voices filling the halls of their home and the glens around the villa.

One afternoon in the summer of 1936, a famous opera singer named Lotte Lehman overheard the family singing in their garden. They had "gold in their throats," she exclaimed. Family choirs were rare. They should give concerts, even go to America!

Maria had never thought of singing professionally. Their evening songfests were held to draw the family closer together . . . and to become closer to God. "When you sing, you pray twice," Maria told the children. But the opera star encouraged them to sing at the upcoming Salzburg Music Festival.

The Music Festival, held every year, was a world-renowned event. The home of Mozart was a natural place for music lovers to gather. Founded in 1920, the summer festival had become an annual event. Activities began in late July and ended in early September. There were operas, puppet shows, concerts, folk dances, and singing. The Von Trapps had attended, but they never dreamed of performing. Maria couldn't face crowds from a stage!

The baron was horrified at the notion of his family appearing on stage. The Von Trapps did not perform in public. But Miss Lehman convinced him to let Maria and the children try out for the amateur group singing contest at the festival.

"Just for this one time," he agreed reluctantly.

Before Maria knew it, she and her family were entered in the amateur contest. During the festival, they were whisked up on the stage in the concert hall. Maria was miserable with stage fright, but somehow they sang three beautiful numbers—and won! The embarrassed baron slipped away before his family received their award.

Next came an opportunity to sing on the radio. Maria didn't want to repeat the agony of the Salzburg contest. But that was not enough of a reason to turn down the offer, and so they sang on the radio program.

Chancellor Schuschnigg, Austria's chief executive, happened to hear the program. He liked their singing so much, he invited the Trapp Family Choir to perform at a state reception in December. Even Georg couldn't refuse a request from the chancellor. Maria and the children performed at the grand event with the famous Vienna Philharmonic Orchestra. Their performance was very well received. When people mentioned trying out for the professional Salzburg Music Festival instead of the amateur group singing contest, Maria became excited. Even Georg lost his pained look.

At the next Salzburg Music Festival, the Trapp Family was the only family choir at the concert. They were a hit. This time, concert managers flocked to them, offering contracts from countless countries, even the United States. Georg pasted their reviews in a scrapbook.

The contracts came in handy. That next year, the Von Trapp family toured Europe. They sang in all the great cities—Paris, London, Rome, and Brussels. They performed before royalty and even the pope. Besides the money, the tour gave them an excellent opportunity to see the rest of Europe. For Maria, seeing famous cathedrals and churches was a dream come true.

German troops march into Austria in March 1938.

Things were going well for Maria and her family, but that winter, the political shadow lengthened with each passing day. On the evening of March 11, 1938, Maria and Georg were listening to the radio in the library when Chancellor Schuschnigg began speaking.

He bade his countrymen farewell. Austria had fallen under the strong force of its powerful neighbor, Germany. Shocked, Maria heard the German anthem pour from the speakers, then the harsh cries of "Heil, Hitler!" Since Salzburg was situated near the border between Austria and Germany, German soldiers quickly invaded the city. Bells pealed from the city's churches, announcing the arrival of Hitler's troops.

Austria was no more.

Adolf Hitler presides over a Nazi rally in Vienna shortly after the German invasion of Austria.

The next day, the flag of Hitler's Third Reich hung from every window in town. People addressed each other with the outstretched arm of Hitler's troops. Georg would not allow the new German flag, the swastika, to be hung from the villa. He refused to perform the Nazi salute, and he shut his ears to the German anthem. Maria was afraid for him, openly defying Hitler's government. It was not easy to ignore Hitler. German soldiers stood on every street corner. An official of the Third Reich came to the villa and ordered Georg to fly the German flag. Still Georg refused.

Next the baron received an order to join the navy as a submarine commander. During World War I, Georg had been a captain in charge of two submarines. At the end of the war, he came home with medals and ribbons. Georg had to admit that he was excited by the opportunity to command a new U-boat. In 1914, submarines were new and crude vessels—Georg's only held five men. Since then, submarines had become bigger, faster, and more powerful.

Maria said nothing. She let him talk through his feelings, silently praying that the will of God would not let them make a poor decision. Eventually Georg realized he would be fighting against his country if he fought for Hitler's Germany. He turned down the commission.

Then came a chilling invitation—to sing at Adolf Hitler's birthday. Maria knew her husband would say no. And she was afraid of what would happen. Georg called the family together. So far they had refused to fly the flag, sing the anthem, say "Heil, Hitler." They could not openly snub Hitler any longer. They could continue living in the villa, he said, and enjoy their comfortable life as Hitler's puppets. Or they could sacrifice material wealth and keep their faith and honor. But they could not do both.

They decided to leave.

5

A Higher Mountain

After a summer of preparation, the family left Austria as quietly as possible to keep from arousing suspicion. In their hiking costumes, as if this were just an ordinary trip, the Von Trapps fled Salzburg on a train bound for St. Georgen, a town in northern Italy.

The group consisted of three adults, counting Father Wasner, and nine young Von Trapps, ranging in age from seven to twenty-seven. Complicating matters, Maria was expecting another baby.

On the Italian side of the Alps, Maria discovered she had packed silly things—five petticoats, ski boots, a teddy bear named Timmy. She had been so distracted by having to leave Austria that she hadn't been able to think straight. But Georg had planned ahead. He had packed his submarine flag, proudly showing the red and white colors of their homeland, and—most important—the scrapbook of contracts from the Salzburg Music Festival.

The very next day, the Austrian border closed. No one could enter or leave the country. It was as if a door had clanged shut behind them. Maria felt the shock of a person who suddenly had no home, no country to return to. Overnight, her status had gone from citizen to refugee. Ahead lay uncertainty. Perhaps this mountain was too big for them to climb.

The baron's navy pension helped pay room and board for the family. But they couldn't live this way indefinitely. They must go to America, Georg insisted. One contract in the scrapbook was from a manager in the United States, Mr. Wagner. Before they left Austria,

The Von Trapps in hiding at a cottage in St. Georgen, Italy

Georg had written to Mr. Wagner, asking him to arrange for them to travel by ship to America. After six weeks of waiting in Italy, the family finally received their tickets.

They boarded the ship the *American Farmer* in October 1938. Maria was excited to be journeying to the promised land. Most of the passengers were Americans going home. The Von Trapp family was a curiosity. The long dirndl skirts, aprons, and headscarves the girls and Maria wore were often mistaken for Dutch or Norwegian outfits.

Soon after departing from the English coast, the small ship sailed into stormy weather and choppy seas. The dining room was nearly empty during mealtimes. Most of the passengers were seasick and remained in their cabins. The Von Trapp family was no exception. Only Georg and Maria stayed on their feet throughout the storm.

"How's Barbara?" the baron would ask his wife.

"Oh, she is fine," Maria would reply.

Since it seemed girls would continue to outnumber boys in their family, Georg had asked if their next daughter could be named Barbara. Maria had agreed. "Barbara" was already proving to be hardy.

When the stormy weather was over and the passengers reappeared, Maria decided she should learn English. Agathe and Rupert had learned the language in school. One of the passengers had given Rupert a copy of *Gone With the Wind,* and he was already reading it. Georg could also speak English. Maria didn't want to depend on her children or her husband to make herself understood. And she had a whole shipful of people to teach her, since most passengers were Americans. Maria optimistically figured she could learn the language on the Atlantic crossing.

Armed with a notebook and pencil, she would point to an object and politely ask an English-speaking passenger, "Please, what is that?" In her Austrian accent, the phrase came out, "Vat is fat?" She jotted the English word using Austrian spelling. The word *knife* would be transcribed as *neiff. Spoon* was *spuhn.* Soon she added phrases to her vocabulary list, such as "How do you do?" and "Thank you very much."

By the time the skyscrapers of New York City appeared on the horizon, Maria was familiar with American currency—pennies, nickels, dimes, quarters, and "bucks"—and a few American songs, such as "My Old Kentucky Home." America, she believed, was a country filled with kind, helpful people. The Von Trapps should have no problem in the New World.

When the Von Trapps arrived in New York City, Mr. Wagner's assistant, Mr. Snowden, was there to help them through immigration. Then the family took several taxis to the Hotel Wellington, where they would be staying. Maria was amazed to learn that they would be on the nineteenth floor! She had never seen such tall buildings in Austria. Would she ever get used to the soaring heights of the skyscrapers?

The next day, Mr. Snowden arrived to escort the family to Mr. Wagner's office. Maria found that something as simple as getting around was an overwhelming experience. Everyone was in a hurry. Taxis zipped around corners, making walking dangerous. Buses lumbered and

New York City's tall skyscrapers and crowded streets bewildered Maria.

trolley cars clanged. Maria could not get used to the constant racket, the speed, the heat. Austria was never this warm and humid, never this noisy.

Maria was frightened by the elevated train on Sixth Avenue. Even worse was the teeth-rattling subway. Then Mr. Snowden took them into Macy's department store, where Maria had to climb on an escalator. She refused, petrified at the sight of the moving staircase.

"Close your eyes, lady, and take a step," someone urged. That advice would come in handy. Maria would try to remember those words whenever she was confronted with a new situation. And she had a feeling she would be confronting quite a few. Maria was beginning to feel that America was like another towering mountain. Would she ever reach the top?

When the family finally arrived at Mr. Wagner's office, they learned that their concert tour would start in one week. Until then, Mr. Wagner agreed to advance money to the Von Trapps for living expenses.

The following week, they discovered the city's delights. Maria was enchanted with drugstores, where a person could buy anything from alarm clocks to pencils, even on a Sunday. Even ordinary sights such as fire escapes, shoeshine thrones, and newsstands caused Maria and her family to stare in amazement.

Being in New York was a great adventure, but Maria wanted to feel more at home in her new country. While the others explored the public library, Radio City Music Hall, and Central Park, Maria decided to stay in the hotel, trying to perfect her English. As soon as she learned the language, she would feel less like a stranger in this new land. She would be able to talk to people, figure out the ways of Americans, and adapt to American life.

Maria pored over menus and labored over an old *Reader's Digest,* aided with a dictionary. She devised her own method of learning grammar. If more than one *mouse* are *mice,* than more than one *house* must be *hice.* Literal translation was also a problem. Once, she tried to translate from her German Bible into English. The sentence was "the spirit is willing, but the flesh is weak." Maria's version came out, "The ghost was willing, but the meat was soft."

As their first week in New York came to a close, the Von Trapps prepared for the concert tour. Rosmarie and Eleonore were too young to take on the road, so Maria and Georg decided to enroll them in boarding school.

The city school was so different from the woods and meadows the little girls had known in Austria. No grass, no trees, only pavement and brick. Leaving her daughters was painful. Maria knew how it felt to be packed off to live with strangers, and her heart broke for her girls. She promised that she would visit them whenever she could.

Soon it was time to leave New York. All of America was out there, ready to be scaled. Maria would need more than five petticoats to tackle this mountain.

6

The Big Blue Bus

The Von Trapps loaded fifty-six pieces of luggage into the coach that announced "Trapp Family Choir." The big blue bus was their new home. Frenchy, their driver, took it upon himself to educate the Austrians on their first American tour. He tooted the horn three times whenever they crossed a new state line and offered commentary about the people and sights.

The bus sped south, heading toward the state of Pennsylvania. Maria was apprehensive about their first concert, which was at Lafayette College in Easton. Would the audience like them? Suppose no one came?

Hours later, when they stepped behind the footlights, Maria realized this college auditorium was a far cry from the majestic Salzburg Music Festival concert hall. Suddenly Maria was aware that she wasn't in another European country, but on a different continent.

In Europe, audiences responded to the Von Trapp's serious music with enthusiasm. But their first performance in the United States was greeted by polite applause.

What went wrong? Maria wondered. Hadn't they sung with genuine emotion? Again she realized that here they were newcomers. Just as it would take some time for the Von Trapps to get used to America, it would take a while for America to get used to them.

Besides lukewarm audiences, they had to endure endless after-concert receptions, where Maria's hand would be squeezed until it was limp. She was often tired. Her back hurt and her ankles swelled, but she smiled and tried to make conversation in her limited English.

Maria's biggest problem was hiding her growing pregnancy. In Austria, a dressmaker had cleverly fashioned a series of undergarments that would make Maria look heavy all over. She hoped American audiences wouldn't mind a stout Mother von Trapp!

Over the years, the Von Trapps toured on several different buses. Each one became a home away from home.

When the big blue bus drove the family into New York City again on the northern leg of their tour, Maria mentioned to their manager that she would be glad when the baby came. She was already in her eighth month. Mr. Wagner was shocked. He had no idea Mrs. von Trapp was expecting. Maria couldn't believe he didn't know! She felt huge.

Mr. Wagner didn't like the idea of Maria performing when she was pregnant. It wouldn't look right, he told them. He immediately canceled the remainder of their concerts. They had only performed eighteen of their forty dates. That meant the family would make less money.

The Von Trapps went back to Hotel Wellington. Now what? They could not perform until after the baby was born. And they had no place to live. It was too expensive for so many people to stay in a hotel. Luckily for the family, they met a music lover who helped them rent a furnished house near Philadelphia. Maria was grateful to have solid flooring under her feet for a change. Best of all, Rosmarie and Eleonore joined them. The whole family was together again.

Word spread that Austrian refugees had moved into the neighborhood. People brought whatever the Von Trapps lacked—linens, pots and pans, even records for the Victrola. That Christmas, they were presented with six turkeys, hams, and lavish baskets of fruit, pies, and cakes. They were also given toys and books for the youngest children. Maria was touched by the generosity of strangers. They would never be poor as long as they had friends.

In January 1939, Maria's baby was born. To everyone's amazement, "Barbara" was a boy. Georg and Maria named their American-born child Johannes Georg.

The Von Trapp family smiles for the camera in 1939. Maria is holding baby Johannes.

Maria learned about American practicality with her new baby. The baby clothes from home were beautiful, delicate dresses. But an American friend scoffed at the lacy outfits. Newborns only needed three knitted shirts, two dozen diapers, and a pair of rubber pants. Maria was astounded. Then she realized she had no baby nurse and no maids to launder and iron the little dresses. Unlike many Austrian women, American women performed these chores themselves. Maria didn't want to be like the other refugees she knew—caught between her homeland and her new home and never accepted in either country. Maria was determined to adopt American ways, starting with her American child.

In February, Mr. Wagner visited the Von Trapps. He brought a new contract for another forty concerts. Their second tour would begin in September. But before the family could get too excited, they received some bad news. The U.S. immigration service informed the Von Trapps their visa was up. The extension they had applied for had been denied. They had to leave the United States immediately.

This was a big blow, and, at first, Maria was afraid. She and her family had started to make a new life in America. She even had an American-born child. They had been through so much already. Could they survive another challenge? Maria knew the answer. She had been forced from her home once before, when she left Nonnberg Abbey to teach the baron's little girl. She had managed then; she would manage once more.

On March 4, 1939, the Von Trapps waved good-bye to

their American friends from the deck of the *Normandie*. Fortunately, Father Wasner had booked them six concerts in Scandinavia. Six concerts would feed the group of twelve plus one baby for about three weeks. After that— well, Maria tried not to fret.

Once they arrived in Europe, Maria did not know from one day to the next whether the family would have enough food or a place to sleep that night. Yet the end of a concert always brought an invitation to perform in another town. When their stay was up in a borrowed house, a friend would lend them another place. Maria learned to relax, realizing that worry only drained energy she could better use for singing or caring for her family.

As the family moved from city to city, Maria saw that the Europe they had left seven months ago had changed. Threat of war hung over the land as Hitler's Germany seemed prepared to invade other neighboring countries. Tourists were viewed with suspicion, as though they might be spies. When Maria and the girls slipped into Austria later that summer, they were greeted coldly. Maria knew her fellow Austrians were angry because they had escaped. Living under the harsh rule of Hitler's Nazi government had hardened her old friends. The Austria she had known was gone. Her home was in America now.

On September 1, 1939, Hitler invaded Poland. This act triggered World War II. Borders slammed shut like iron gates. The Von Trapps had been booked to perform in Sweden. Concerts were canceled and foreigners were ordered home. Fortunately, Mr. Wagner wired them passage on the SS *Bergensfjord*. This ship was a far cry from the luxury of the *Normandie,* but Maria would have floated across the Atlantic on a raft.

When the ship docked in Brooklyn, New York, on October 7, 1939, Mr. Snowden was waiting on the pier to welcome them home. But first the family would have to go through immigration once again. Rupert had obtained an immigration visa, but the rest of the family only had visitors' visas. Maria was so glad to be back in the United States, she paid little attention to the routine examination by the immigration officer.

Suddenly the officer became very serious. The family was questioned repeatedly. By this time, all the other passengers had left the ship. Only the Von Trapp family remained. The next day, everyone but Rupert was shipped to nearby Ellis Island prison.

The prison warden warned the family against discussing their problems with other prisoners, but talkative Maria had already made several friends. Information from the other inmates was more helpful than the terse orders issued from the warden. Maria learned that some families had been detained as long as eight months. The Von Trapps couldn't possibly stay that long—their first concert was on the fifteenth! And they still didn't know why they were there!

Life on Ellis Island was grim. Dormitory doors were locked with a special key. Bright lights shined all night. At mealtimes, the inmates lined up two by two. A large woman poked them each on the shoulder, counting them. This irritated Georg more than anything. They ate at long tables, their food lumped on tin plates.

Immigration officers at Ellis Island kept careful records of each new immigrant. A person had to have the proper documents, answer questions correctly, and have a clean bill of health to be allowed into the United States.

After lunch, the inmates could go out into the yard, two at a time. Maria gazed through the tall wire fence at the Statue of Liberty. Freedom was so near and yet so far!

The Von Trapp family whiled away the long hours by rehearsing and watching Johannes, who had learned to walk. The other inmates enjoyed their concerts.

Then Rupert arrived with the bad news. When the immigration officer had asked how long the family was planning to stay in the United States, someone in their group had remarked that he or she never wanted to leave the United States. The correct response should have been the time stated on their visas, six months.

Maria suddenly remembered her impulsive comment to the immigration officer. When the immigration officer asked Maria how long she intended to stay in the United States, she had blurted, "Oh, I am so glad to be here—I never want to leave again!" She hadn't meant to get them in trouble. She was simply overjoyed and had said the first thing that popped into her mind. Rupert reassured her that the family's American friends were working hard to free them.

A hearing was scheduled on the fourth day of their stay on Ellis Island. For more than two hours, the entire family, especially Maria, was questioned in detail. The judge demanded to know why she had said she never wanted to leave when she had a six-month visa. Maria explained over and over that her remark was made in a rash moment, but the judge didn't believe her.

After the hearing, Maria felt like crying. She had gotten her family into a terrible mess! Instead of crying, the Von Trapps did what they did best as a group—they sang. In the middle of a song, Georg's name rang out in the echoing hall. Someone had come to tell Georg that the family was free! Their friends had come through for them, writing and calling senators and congressmen. The other detainees clapped. This was the sweetest applause Maria had ever heard. She couldn't wait to climb on the big blue bus again.

7

From Baroness to Pioneer

The Von Trapps' second tour was marked by discouragingly small audiences. Maria knew Americans were anxious about the war in Europe, but people always needed music in their lives. It frustrated Maria that there was little or no publicity to announce the concerts. Mr. Wagner seemed to think people who had never heard of the Trapp Family Choir would magically appear on performance night.

Before each concert, Mr. Wagner sent a letter on pink stationery reminding the Von Trapps how many seats were empty at the last performance. As the tour progressed, the number of pink envelopes increased.

What were they doing wrong? Maria wondered. They rehearsed endlessly, added more difficult pieces to their repertoire, and smiled bravely during after-concert receptions. The pink envelopes and half-filled concert halls made them discouraged and anxious.

Maria tried to remember what she had learned time and time again. Just like her first ride on an escalator, she had to shut her eyes and keep taking steps forward. This was simply another mountain to scale. And, besides, it didn't make sense to waste time worrying when there were so many exciting things to see in America.

The Von Trapp family enjoyed seeing the lush scenery of the southern states, the neat farms of Pennsylvania, and the gentle Blue Ridge Mountains of Virginia. On the last lap of the tour, they traveled through New England. Maria was struck by the beauty of Vermont. The snow-covered mountains reminded her of home.

On the road, Maria snapped photos of anything that interested her: Burma Shave signs, Coca-Cola billboards, factories, filling stations, parking lots, and people. And she asked Frenchy questions about everything she saw. Every day brought a new town and new experiences. Maria believed they were meant to be in America, no matter what. It seemed to be God's will that the Trapp Family Choir bring the beauty of music to the people of this country.

Then came the blow. When Georg and Maria went to see their manager in New York, Mr. Wagner starkly reported the amount of money he had lost on them. "You will never be a hit in America," he told them. "Go back to Europe. You will be a success there."

But they couldn't go back to Europe, where Hitler ruled.

Maria and Georg's American friends believed steadfastly in the family's talent. One friend offered to rent cheaply to them a house near Philadelphia, in a town called Merion. Maria liked the white house with blue shutters. After so many months of living in hotels, it was heaven to have a place to call home. In a real house, she had a chance to think about their situation. Maria decided it was time to find a new manager.

But how did one find a new manager? A friend suggested that Maria simply phone a respected manager and ask for an audition. Maria remembered meeting a manager at a party who seemed to care for his clients. She phoned F. C. Schang. With that simple telephone call, the Von Trapps had an audition. They would perform for Mr. Schang in one week.

In December 1939, the Von Trapps walked into Steinway Hall for their audition. They sang their most impressive pieces by the famous European composers Bach and Palestrina. But Mr. Schang shook his head after their performance. He didn't want them.

Maria knew that the family could audition for other managers. But she firmly believed that Mr. Schang was the best manager for them. And once Maria got an idea in her head, it was hard to dislodge the notion. The Trapp Family Choir would be Mr. Schang's new clients, one way or another.

Maria went to see Mr. Schang alone and demanded to know why they had been rejected. Mr. Schang told her the scalding truth. Their program was too serious and too long for the average American audience. The quaint musical instruments were ridiculous. Worst of all was their overall appearance. They were too solemn and their costumes were ugly.

The Von Trapp girls in the traditional Austrian clothing that F. C. Schang
disliked so much

When Mr. Schang suggested that Maria and the girls wear shorter skirts, nylon stockings, and makeup, she bristled. She felt that Mr. Schang had completely misunderstood her family as artists. But her English was not good enough to express her anger. Instead she picked up a book from his desk and slammed it down.

"I thinked," she stated, "America free country. *Is not!*"

Mr. Schang admired Maria's spunk. After some thought, he agreed to represent the Von Trapps for one season, but only if there were some changes, starting with their name. The Trapp Family Choir sounded too religious. Instead, they would be called the Trapp Family Singers.

The Von Trapps would start touring for Columbia Concerts in September 1940, with a break after Christmas. Until then they were free, but there was plenty to do in their new home. Because of the war in Europe, their visas were extended. No one would make the Von Trapps return to Nazi-occupied Austria. Without constant uncertainty dogging her, Maria decided it was time to make the white house with blue shutters a real home.

Everyone had assigned chores: Johanna ran the kitchen, Hedwig did the laundry, Agathe sewed, young Maria mended their clothes and darned the woolen stockings, and the boys washed the dishes. Georg did the shopping, while Father Wasner handled the accounts. Maria took care of correspondence and continued to learn American ways.

Betty, a neighbor, was shocked by Maria's slangy English. A baroness should not say "jeepers creepers," "guys," or "shucks," and she most definitely should not tell someone to "jump in the lake." Maria tried to re-member, but what else could she say when she wanted to tell someone to jump in the lake?

Maria also had problems with housework. In Europe, even modest households had a servant to help with the ironing or heavy cleaning. But in America, women did housework themselves. At first, Maria ducked out the back door when friends stopped by, so they would not catch her scrubbing the floor.

Maria slowly realized that work was what had built the United States into such a great country. People who came here were free to do anything they pleased—but they had to do it themselves. Maria could relate to that. She re-membered how she had turned the Von Trapp villa into a boardinghouse when the bank failed in Austria. She had helped clean and wash the linens—something unheard of for a lady of her station. Her pioneer spirit rallied in America, too. Work was nothing to be ashamed of.

When Father Wasner announced one day that they had less than fifty dollars in the bank and four months until their next concert date, Maria had an idea. She had seen an exhibit of Pennsylvania Dutch handicrafts. Why couldn't the Von Trapps sell some of their own crafts? After all, they had been making Christmas and birthday presents for each other for years.

Within two weeks, their home was wall-to-wall with items to sell: furniture by Georg, beautifully painted trays and wooden bowls from Martina's brush, clay sculptures by Johanna, linoleum cuts by Agathe, artistic carvings by young Maria, leatherwork by Hedwig, and jewelry made by Werner. Maria and Rupert weren't artistic, so they did the selling. Their show was such a success, they gave another in New York. Soon orders poured in. Maria knew that they could always use their hands when they couldn't sing. She also learned that America was truly the land of opportunity.

When September finally came, the family prepared to leave Merion to tour with Columbia Concerts. Mr. Schang advised the family to smile and relax on stage. He also mentioned that their performance lacked something. He didn't know what it was, but he knew Maria would figure it out.

On their third tour, days passed in a blur of new places, new songs to learn, and a new bed every night. When they arrived in New Mexico or California or Washington, they checked into the cheapest hotel, unloaded all their luggage, rehearsed, performed, and toppled into bed. The next day, the whole process started over.

Life on the bus brought its own problems. Audiences saw the Von Trapp family singing together in perfect harmony. But living in a cramped, jostling bus caused more than a few sour notes.

One morning, Maria was late checking out of the hotel. Frenchy blew his horn impatiently. Someone had taken someone else's seat. Nothing was right about the day. Soon everyone was arguing and complaining. Finally Georg ordered silence. Then he told them that a situation called a *tropenkoller* had taken over the bus. He had seen it happen many times. When people are in close quarters too long, trivial incidents trigger arguments. Maria knew what he meant—if one of the children slouched, or one cleared his throat too often, or another looked sloppy, she was annoyed.

At least the concerts were going better on this tour. But Maria still had not figured out the missing ingredient that would make the Trapp Family Singers a success. Generally the family stuck to the program arranged by Father Wasner. Maria made a point of stating at the beginning of every concert, "A family which sings together, plays together, and prays together usually stays together." She believed in that statement, and it set the tone for the program.

When the Trapp Family Singers performed, Maria could feel that the audience was "thirsty for beauty."

In Denver, Colorado, Maria decided to try something new. She wanted to close the show with a number that was not in the program. Stepping forward, she announced a yodeling song. Yodeling requires a singer to draw in a lungful of air to sing a long pattern of high and low notes. As Maria took a deep breath, a fly flew into her mouth! She couldn't cough up the fly on-stage. Choking and turning purple, Maria felt she must apologize to the audience.

"What has never happened before, has happened now," she admitted. "I swallowed a fly."

To her surprise, everyone laughed. They understood! Maria went on to translate the story of the Austrian folk song, using a word that meant "underwear" when she meant to say "goatskin." Again everyone laughed.

Maria realized they weren't laughing at her, but with her. She had established a link with the audience. After-ward, people remarked that she had made them feel at home. Maria had figured out the "something" their per-formance lacked. From then on, the Trapp Family Singers would make their audiences feel like one big family.

Their purpose for being in America, for climbing on the bus and onstage, was to sing. Singing had brought them together as a family. Sharing their talent would bring the Von Trapps and their audiences together as a family, too. It was their mission.

8

A Mountain of Her Own

A poster from late 1941 triumphantly announced that the Trapp Family Singers had broken all records during that concert season. The next year, the Von Trapps performed ninety-six concerts, and the third year under Columbia's management, over one hundred dates were booked.

The Trapp Family Singers were Freddy Schang's most successful act. They had improved their program by including familiar American folk songs as well as classical music. Their stage presence was more cheerful, and the girls now wore shorter skirts and makeup. In the first half of their act, the Von Trapp girls wore white silk gowns. Maria's gown was black taffeta. The boys came onstage in black suits. After the classical selections, the family played various instruments: recorders, the spinet, the viola de gamba. Then there was an intermission. When the curtain drew back once more, the Von Trapps were wearing Austrian costumes—the girls dressed in dirndl skirts, aprons, and puff-sleeved blouses, the boys in their Austrian shorts, stockings, and silver-buckled shoes. And as always, Maria charmed her audience with her stories.

At the end of their fifth touring year, the Von Trapps had paid their debts and had some money left over. Though they were grateful to return to the house with the blue shutters after traveling, the hot summers in Pennsylvania were difficult. Being Austrian, the Von Trapps were accustomed to cooler climates. And they all longed to go hiking as they had done in Austria. For the first time, they could afford to go on a real vacation. But where could they go?

When a friend offered the family a tourist house in Stowe, Vermont, Maria remembered the beauty of Vermont and the mountains that had reminded her of Austria. The Von Trapps decided to pack their two automobiles and drive north. They spent a wonderful summer in Stowe, hiking, picnicking, and swimming. They even gave an army benefit concert at an old Conservation Civilian Corps (CCC) camp. Singing outdoors under the stars was magical. Maria thought they had never sounded better. She dreaded the day they would have to leave. If only they could buy a place in the country!

Then Maria learned they could buy a farm. Amazingly, it was cheaper to buy a farm than a house. Since all family decisions were made democratically, they voted on whether to spend the extra money on new clothes or a farm.

Store-bought clothes would cost five hundred dollars per person, and anyway, everyone in America was used to seeing them in their native costumes. Agathe would sew them new outfits. That decided, they began looking for the perfect farm to fulfill their hearts' desire.

The place that captured Maria's heart wasn't exactly perfect. The farmhouse and outbuildings were falling down, Georg pointed out practically. But the view! From the sunbathed peaks, they could see three valleys lying placidly between ancient mountain ranges. She would never tire of the view—the mountains, woods, pastures, and miles of open sky reminded her of Austria. And she did not want to live in Merion forever. The suburbs, she realized, were not for her.

But Georg was reluctant to sign on the dotted line. Maria understood his caution—he didn't want to make a costly mistake. Yet hadn't all their risks paid off so far? "Oh, Georg," she told him, "we can build a house and barns, but we can never build a view like this!" Days later, the entire family crowded into the town clerk's office to sign the deed. They owned nearly seven hundred acres of unspoiled countryside.

On the road for another tour, the Von Trapps read agriculture pamphlets and discussed what to do with the farm. As always, each member had a different idea. Martina wanted to raise pigs, and Hedwig voted for cows. Young Maria thought they should grow vegetables, while Agathe wanted to keep bees. Johanna cast her vote for sheep. Father Wasner was all for an orchard. Maria wanted to raise horses.

Stowe, Vermont

Only the boys were silent. Then they broke the news: they had been drafted by the U.S. government to serve in the army to fight the war in Europe. Rupert was thirty-one and Werner was twenty-seven.

In the late winter of 1943, Rupert and Werner left for Camp Hale in Colorado. They had volunteered for the Mountain Troops. Maria wondered how the family could perform without the boys. Their entire musical program had been built around mixed voices. Father Wasner re-arranged several of their old numbers and added new songs designed for women's choirs.

Maria missed the boys terribly and didn't like performing without them. But she felt that her family's concerts were part of the war effort, and she wanted to support Americans any way she could. The more she read the newspapers, the more she was thankful her family was in America. Here they were free to work at a profession they loved and say whatever they felt.

It was March 1943 when the family moved to their farmhouse in Stowe. Snow lay in deep drifts. The ramshackle farmhouse, which had seemed quaint earlier that summer, was much too small for their large family. All they needed to do, a local architect breezily assured them, was raise the roof and add another story.

With the help of a carpenter, Georg, young Maria, and Hedwig tore off most of the roof. Snow filtered into the

Maria always stressed the importance of family unity and teamwork. Here the Von Trapps work together on their farm in Stowe.

living room. As much as Maria loved nature, she didn't care for it inside her house. Then a blizzard struck. What was left of the roof and floor crashed to the cellar under the weight of snow. It was clear that the old house just wouldn't suit. They would have to tear down the entire house and build a new one.

Georg worried about the expense, but Maria reminded him that a nation is worth as much as it is willing to work. That applied to their family as well, which meant the Von Trapps were worth a fortune. Somehow, they would find a way to build a new home.

Maria and Georg asked an architect to design the house of their dreams, an Austrian chalet. Until then, the family would have to make do. They would live in the barn and camp in tents until the new house was built. It would be another adventure!

Spring arrived in a tumble of flowers, bugs, and wild animals. Maria discovered their "open" living arrangement had its drawbacks. One afternoon she was startled by a skunk that had decided to settle under the icebox.

Georg, Hedwig, and twenty-eight-year-old Maria formed the Von Trapp family construction crew. The others dug ditches and mixed cement. Agathe tended the beehives, Martina fed the pigs, Maria weeded the garden, and Hedwig washed clothes in an outdoor laundry.

The days passed in a blur. Maria was barely aware that a reporter and photographer had come to do a story on the Von Trapp's new life. She allowed them to tag after her, but she had no time for posing. It was haying season and she was busy driving Lady and Prince, the horses.

Later that summer, Rupert and Werner came home on their first leave from the army. Now the whole family worked on the house. Soon the first floor was up. When the boys went back to Colorado, the roof had been started. But because of the war, there were few men to hire to finish the job. And money was tight, as always. Maria worried their house wouldn't be ready for winter. Then the family had a stroke of luck.

Maria had heard the Stowe school needed a new roof. The family offered to put on a concert to raise funds. The concert was a big success. More important than earning money for a new schoolhouse roof, the Von Trapps earned a place in the community.

A few days later, pickup trucks rumbled up the road. The high school shop teacher had gathered all available young men. The boys worked the next two days. When they were finished, the roof was shingled, doors and windows were set in the walls, and the outside was tar papered. The Trapp Family Singers left on their fall tour, secure in the knowledge that the townspeople of Stowe would welcome them home.

As soon as the concert season was over, they returned to work on their house. One day a friend told them the old CCC camp where the Von Trapps had sung for the army was going to be torn down. Maria remembered the gravel-pit outdoor theater and how beautiful their voices had sounded. It would be a shame to tear down the camp, conveniently located at the bottom of their hill.

She asked the state forester in charge of the camp to visit them. Suppose the Von Trapps bought the camp?

Rosmarie and Eleonore von Trapp walk toward the family's newly built home in Stowe.

she ventured. What would they do with a camp? Maria was asked. Yes, the expressions in her family's eyes seemed to say. What *would* we do with a camp?

Maria thought. And then she knew how they would use the camp.

Often on their travels, people asked the Von Trapps why they never sang anything modern. Maria would reply that America was so rich with folk music from every region, why bother with popular tunes anyone could hear on the radio? A music camp would be a way to bring more of that music to the people. She would model her camp on the Sing Weeks she had attended when she was young. She and her friends spent a week or more learning folk dances and singing. Nowhere in America was there a place devoted to music making.

Her family stared at her. Maria knew they were wondering what she was dragging them into this time. They probably didn't need another project. But Maria enjoyed a life filled to the brim. And she couldn't bear the thought of a perfectly good camp going to waste.

Everyone agreed at least to go down the hill to inspect the property. The camp consisted of eleven barracks, a kitchen and dining room, and a recreation hall. Even Georg admitted the buildings were well constructed. After looking over the grounds, four-year-old Johannes pointed to a rainbow arching through the sky.

"Let's take this rainbow for a good sign," Maria said to her husband.

The state of Vermont agreed to lease the camp to the family for ten years. Suddenly they were in the summer camp business.

While touring, Maria began planning ahead for the camp. On the bus and in hotel rooms, Maria made lists of things they needed for 120 people: beds, linens, toilets, pillows, spoons. It was like furnishing the Trapp family house ten times over! The Von Trapps also sent out flyers advertising their music camp and spoke about the camp to audiences. By the time they had finished their long West Coast tour, 104 people had made reservations.

They arrived home on May 24. The camp would officially open on July 10, 1944. They had just forty-six days to convert abandoned army barracks into guest cottages. There was no time to waste. Maria scoured secondhand stores and auctions for washbowls, blankets, lumber, and hot-water tanks. The family worked around the clock, painting and scrubbing the dormitories, which were named after composers such as Beethoven, Schubert, and Mozart.

Finally the first Trapp Family Music Camp was under way. For ten days, campers sang by the brook and under the trees. They danced on the lawn and sang outdoors and discussed music and life deep into the night. There were field trips to the peak of nearby Mount Mansfield and to a lake, with picnic lunches and more music.

A tireless hostess, Maria was everywhere at once. She was delighted to bring classical works to people who had never sung before. Even more important, their ten-day course gave families an opportunity to sing together. She was thrilled that other families could experience what the Von Trapps lived on a daily basis. One voice was beautiful, but many voices made life stronger and richer.

9

Many Hands, One Heart

The big bell in the music camp rang with the glad news. It was August 1945, and the news spread through the second Trapp Family Music Camp like the ringing of the bell—the war in Europe was finally over. Rupert and Werner would soon return from Italy, where they had been stationed.

With the family all together again, they resumed touring. Now they had a big blue-and-cream-colored bus outfitted with a cot and eating area. The youngest children, Johannes, Eleonore, and Rosmarie, went, too, and had their lessons on the road.

People recognized the Von Trapps everywhere they went. They had been featured in many newspapers and magazines, including *Life*. Total strangers inquired about Johannes, who had appeared in a photograph with Maria. Maria wasn't shy about being in the limelight. She was proud of her family and their accomplishments.

The Von Trapp family on tour in San Francisco in 1946. Pictured are (BACK ROW, LEFT TO RIGHT) Eleonore, Werner, Maria, Johannes, Martina, Rosmarie and (FRONT ROW) Johanna, Hedwig, Father Wasner, Georg, Maria, and Agathe.

After the war, the Von Trapps used their fame to aid fellow Austrians. The Trapp Family Austrian Relief Fund collected food, clothing, and donations to send to war-torn Austria. Maria appealed to concert audiences for help. Donations were then loaded in their big bus and shipped back to the farm in Stowe. Once more, the Von Trapps worked together as a team. On the bus, the Von Trapp women packed boxes, while others wrote labels and tied the boxes for mailing. Maria answered letters balancing a typewriter on her lap.

Again she was impressed by American generosity. A woman came up to her after a concert and gave Maria the coat off her back. She was a teacher and hoped her coat would go to a teacher in Austria. Altogether, the Von Trapps sent 275,000 pounds of goods back to their homeland.

Everything seemed to be going well for Maria and her family. But a second lengthy, postwar tour, combined with the efforts of the relief fund, took its toll. Georg became ill. Though he attended the concerts, he spent more time resting on the cot in the back of the bus.

Maria urged her husband to fly back to New York, where he was hospitalized for pneumonia. Worried, Maria flew to New York to be with him. There she learned the worst: Georg had lung cancer. She took her husband home to the farm. The rest of the family returned when the tour was over, so they had a little time to spend with their father. The baron passed away on May 30, 1947. Maria was with him at the end.

Maria spent the month of June lost in grief and feelings of regret. Though she and Georg had loved each other, they had opposite temperaments. Maria's short fuse caused her to explode and sometimes even throw things in anger, while Georg preferred to talk over disagreements. Now Maria regretted her stormy, childish behavior. If only she could relive those days, she would be much kinder to her husband.

Maria's biggest problem was to get through the next camp season. She had to put on the bright, cheerful face of the magazine photos and endure insensitive remarks about Georg's death. At night, she gave in to her grief and cried. Finally she went to see a psychiatrist. When this doctor was no help, Maria went to a priest. She told him everything that had been troubling her. At the confession, the priest said that both God and Georg had forgiven her.

Maria learned to accept the death of her husband, but it seemed her family was falling apart. First, eighteen-year-old Rosmarie wandered away from home. The strain of her father's death, added to the long tour and getting ready for high school graduation, was too much for her. For three days and nights, people searched the woods and fields around the area. Finally Maria informed the media, unable to put off the reporters any longer. Rosmarie was found in a pasture, unhurt. But she was depressed for many months afterward.

Next, eight-year-old Johannes came down with rheumatic fever. These were the days when polio filled every parent's heart with fear. Johannes had to stay in bed for several weeks. Hedwig, age thirty, was ill also. Then Eleonore was hit by a truck, though she was not seriously hurt.

On top of it all, Maria miscarried a baby that September. Afterward an old kidney problem flared and she remained bedridden, too sad and too sick to attend Rupert's wedding. Rupert had completed his American degree in medicine and had become a doctor before his father died. He married Henriette Lajoie, whom he'd met at one of their summer camps.

Eventually Maria recovered from her illness, but she had to drop out of the fall concert tour and was once again hospitalized. The following year, 1948, Maria received devastating news—she had a brain tumor. Her doctors must operate, even though she had a fifty-fifty chance of recovery.

Maria's first thought was of her family. What would happen to them if she didn't make it? By now, both Rupert and Johanna were married. She knew that some of the other children would marry as well. With the members of her family striking out on their own, she had to hire outside singers for their group. How long could they continue to tour? What could the rest of the family do to make a living?

A concerned friend suggested that Maria turn the Von Trapp home into a ski lodge. Why not take advantage of the great ski weather in Stowe? If she turned the farmhouse into a lodge, the family would have another source of income.

Maria gave the idea some thought. It was true that "leftover" guests from the music camp summers—husbands who didn't sing or people who dropped in unexpectedly—had become a fixture in the chalet. Since the family lived down the hill while camp was in session, they rented their bedrooms to the extra people. Guests loved the place so much, they even asked if they could rent rooms while the Von Trapp family was on tour. Maybe the idea of a lodge would work. And the Von Trapps had recently sold their villa in Austria, so they had money to build onto their farmhouse.

Luckily Maria's operation was a success. The family could continue to perform, but Maria still wanted to open a lodge. A new wing was added to the main house, using money from the sale of the villa. When the new guest rooms weren't adequate, another wing was built. A cook and a housekeeper completed the staff. The family decided their home needed a name. Father Wasner suggested Cor Unum, Latin words meaning "One Heart." The Trapp Family Lodge was born.

With one heart, the Von Trapps officially became U.S. citizens in May 1948. After nearly ten years in America, the Von Trapps were truly Americans. The family dropped the *von* from their names. They were simply the Trapps.

Life finally seemed to be settling down for Maria, but Maria wasn't interested in settling down. Always on the lookout for a new project, she decided to write a book about the Trapp Family Singers. She got the idea from a publisher named Bert Lippincott.

Mr. Lippincott had gone to see a Trapp Family Singers concert in Philadelphia and was impressed by Maria's storytelling ability. After the concert, the publisher raced backstage to ask Maria to write down her stories.

Her tales would make a fascinating book. Maria agreed. Ever since the fly incident in Denver, she'd had plenty of practice holding an audience's attention.

Maria dictated the book to her secretary but ran over the word limit by fifty thousand words. Maria simply kept the extra length for a sequel. *The Story of the Trapp Family Singers* was published in 1949. Maria's book told the saga of their remarkable family. The book won the Catholic Writers Book Award and was translated into several languages, including German. People related to the romantic, exciting story of an orphan girl who became a baron's wife and later turned her refugee family into an international music group.

Then a Hollywood film company offered to purchase film rights to the book. Maria was concerned they might change her story. When the producer said he only wanted to use the title and planned to write an entirely different screenplay, Maria turned down the offer.

Americans loved reading about Maria and her family, but meanwhile the family continued to change. Along with Rupert and Johanna, Werner and Martina had also gotten married. Maria knew she couldn't hang on to the children forever. They were adults, with their own lives ahead of them. Yet each one who left took a part of Cor Unum with him or her.

The Trapp Family Singers had also changed. Werner and Martina still sang with the group, but Rupert was working in a hospital as a doctor and Johanna quit singing to be a diplomat's wife. Rosmarie had stage fright and would not be touring anymore. A tenor replaced Rupert. Eleven-year-old Johannes was singing as a soprano.

The group's concerts were expanding beyond American shores. In 1950, the Trapps toured Mexico, Central and South America, and the Caribbean. The family on wheels became a family on wings as they flew from country to country. They explored a jungle in Brazil, shared a stage in Cuba with cats and dogs, and met a Jesuit priest who kept poisonous snakes. Johannes collected unusual souvenirs: a blowgun with poisonous darts, a headhunter's club, and the largest, hairiest spider Maria had ever seen.

After that lengthy tour, they were invited to sing in the Salzburg Music Festival. To go home after twelve years! Maria recalled that terrible trip just before the war, when friends had treated them like traitors. But this time, things were different. The Trapps were heroes. The

The Trapp Family Singers toured Hawaii in 1955. Professional singers had replaced family members who no longer performed with the choir.

Trapp Family Austrian Relief Fund had helped thousands of Austrians. Every one of them, Maria felt, was waiting when their train pulled into the station. She couldn't believe all those people had come just to see them.

After a flood of welcoming speeches, bouquets, and songs, a bus took them out of the city to Aigen. Soon they were at the Trapp villa, which had become a religious seminary. The seminary students were away on vacation, and the Trapps had been invited to stay in their old home.

After spending time revisiting the old Trapp villa, the younger family members eagerly went out to visit friends and relatives. But Maria stayed home, wanting solitude.

As she stepped into the great hall, a wave of memories washed over her. The Captain's U-boat flag was gone—he had taken it with him when they left. But the life-sized portrait of him in his naval uniform hung on the wall. Maria remembered seeing her husband in his uniform on their wedding day. So much had happened since that day . . . .

When the family came back, Maria was happy to hear their laughing voices. It was time to move forward—time to scale the next mountain.

10

Farewell Song

Maria stood onstage for the final Town Hall concert, gazing out into the audience.

It was December 1955. The Trapp family had spent an incredibly busy year. In May, they toured New Zealand in a whirlwind ten weeks. From there, they toured Australia, covering the vast distances between towns in another blue bus. Soon they were winging home again for their farewell U.S. concert tour. The tour was short, ending, as always, in New York City for the Town Hall Christmas concert.

It had been a tough decision to make, but Maria knew touring had become too difficult for her family. Most of her children were married with families of their own or had developed other interests. Hedwig and Agathe both wanted to teach.

As Maria stood on the stage, she recalled that first Town Hall concert in 1938. The next day's newspapers had declared that the Trapps were "like no other singing family alive." In twenty years, they had given more than two thousand concerts worldwide. And each concert held many memories. Maria remembered the Christmas when pigtailed Eleonore and Rosmarie played their recorders for the first time. And she could almost hear Martina's sweet voice. Martina had died in childbirth four years earlier and was buried beside her father on the grounds of the Trapp home.

And now, with one last bow, it was over.

Maria was never one to dwell on the past. Not while so much had to be done. After she stopped touring as a musician, Maria focused much of her energy on the Trapp Family Lodge. She even opened the Trapp Family Gift Shop.

In the spring of 1956, Johannes, Rosmarie, and young Maria went to the South Sea island of New Guinea as missionaries. They believed that it wasn't enough to send checks to these remote regions. The people needed doctors, teachers, carpenters, and the word of God. Maria had always wanted to travel to the South Seas. After her children left, Maria and Father Wasner toured the South Sea Islands for a year. While in New Guinea, Maria received a letter from the United States. Someone wanted to make a Broadway musical out of her book, *The Story of the Trapp Family Singers,* starring Mary Martin.

A German film about the family, *Die Trapp Family,* (*The Trapp Family*) had been released in Europe. A German movie company had purchased film rights for a sum of ten thousand dollars, payable within a year. At the time, Maria agreed to take a ten percent reduction, making the fee nine thousand dollars, to be paid immediately. There were always outstanding bills. She hadn't understood then that she had given up rights to her own story. And now someone wanted to make a musical. Maria tore the letter into shreds. The idea of their family's story on a Broadway stage was ridiculous!

But when Maria's ship docked weeks later in San Francisco, she was met by Mary Martin's husband. He invited Maria to see Mary Martin in the musical *Annie Get Your Gun.* Maria went and enjoyed the performance. At least she knew who Mary Martin was, but she still couldn't picture a Broadway star playing Maria von Trapp. Producer Leland Hayward convinced Maria that the earnings from the play would pay for the Trapp family's mission work in the South Seas.

Maria learned that the famous Broadway songwriting team of Rodgers and Hammerstein was rewriting her book into a musical script. This was to be their last work together. As production got under way, Mary Martin spent ten days at the lodge with Maria to learn her ways. Maria was amused by the actress imitating her long stride and active hand motions.

Maria attended opening night, on November 16, 1959, wearing a pale green gown and matching shoes that Mary Martin had sent as a gift. The play made some changes

Mary Martin in the original Broadway production of THE SOUND OF MUSIC

from Maria's book. The children's names were changed. Rupert, the oldest, became "Liesl," a girl, and the captain was portrayed as a stern, distant man. But Maria thought Mary Martin had captured the young, impulsive girl she had been, and she was the first to lead the standing ovation.

Despite the initial reviews, which declared the musical to be "too sweet," audiences filled the theater night after night. *The Sound of Music* ran for four and a half years, proof that people loved the heartwarming story of one remarkable family's faith and strength. Songs like "Climb Ev'ry Mountain" and "The Sound of Music" quickly became classics.

A few years later, Hollywood came knocking again. While the Broadway people had asked for Maria's advice, Hollywood baldly told her they were making their own version of her story. She tried to convince the producers not to make her husband as stern as the play version, but they didn't listen.

The film version of *The Sound of Music,* starring Julie Andrews as Maria and Christopher Plummer as the captain, premiered in 1965. The Twentieth Century Fox production remained in theaters for more than four years and won five Academy Awards, including Best Picture.

During the filming of THE SOUND OF MUSIC, Maria met the man who would play her husband—actor Christopher Plummer (RIGHT).

Julie Andrews played a sweet and spunky Maria von Trapp in the film version of THE SOUND OF MUSIC.

Although some critics felt the movie was too sugar-coated, audiences flocked to the theaters, making the movie as popular as the play. When Maria finally saw the movie, she felt that Julie Andrews made her sweeter than she really was. But she was delighted with the opening sequence, a panoramic view of Julie Andrews on a mountaintop. It allowed everyone who saw the movie to appreciate the beauty of her homeland. And Maria, forever the performer, had landed a small role in the movie. Maria, Rosmarie, and her granddaughter Barbara can be seen strolling in the background during Julie Andrews's "I Have Confidence" number.

Although the movie earned millions of dollars, the family received very little, due to Maria's signing away the film rights to the German company. But her family never held her mistake against her.

The Sound of Music made Maria and her family more famous than ever. Maria had become so recognizable that she was stopped on the street wherever she went. People wanted to talk to the woman who had inspired them with her amazing life story.

Maria continued to write about her life, publishing *Around the Years with the Trapp Family; A Family on Wheels; Yesterday, Today, and Forever; Maria;* and *When the King Was Carpenter.* She also traveled the country, speaking on a wide range of topics.

When Maria became ill in Europe on a buying trip for the gift shop, Johannes made her realize she could not continue to do everything. He convinced her to let him take over running the lodge. From her hospital bed,

Maria agreed. But once back home, she reconsidered. Johannes was young and had little experience.

Maria's reason for maintaining control of the lodge was simple: family. She wanted her guests and employees to be an extension of the Trapp family, with everyone happy and getting along. But families aren't businesses and the lodge was losing money. In the end, Maria realized that she had once made her mistakes, and it was time to let Johannes make his.

Maria spent her final years answering the hundreds of letters she received, working in her gift shop, and tending the small cemetery, where her daughter Hedwig was buried with Georg and Martina. Hedwig had moved to Austria to teach. The clear air was supposed to help her asthma. But at age fifty-five, Hedwig died while visiting an aunt.

On March 28, 1987, at the age of eighty-two, the baroness Maria von Trapp died of heart failure. She left behind eight children, twenty-nine grandchildren, and thousands of grateful people whose lives she touched through music.

Maria proved to be an accomplished performer, a successful businesswoman, a fine writer, and a devoted wife and mother. The impulsive girl became a strong woman, capable of facing any adversity. Neither her warm heart nor her courageous spirit will be forgotten.

Maria von Trapp, 1905-1987

Interpreting a Life

I first encountered Maria von Trapp through *The Sound of Music*. I was twelve when the movie came out. That summer, I tried to recreate Maria's fairy-tale life. I even trailed yards of lace from my head, pretending to be a bride solemnly marching down the aisle of Nonnberg Abbey.

Years later, I discovered that Maria von Trapp had written books about her life. I read them, wondering how the Maria in the musical would compare to the real Maria.

To my delight, I found that Maria's life after the Von Trapps left Austria—the point where the movie ended—was even more exciting. Maria's books are humorous, warmhearted, and spirited, as Maria herself was.

Maria led a full, rich life that spilled over into five books. She wrote with typical exuberance, dictating while traveling on the bus, working between the demands of her busy career.

Her books reveal intimate thoughts and feelings not portrayed in the musical. One poignant example occurs when Maria writes about the weeks following the baron's death.

Maria frankly expressed remorse over the times she'd lost her temper with her husband. Her sorrow is painfully evident.

When I began researching my book, I naturally used much of Maria's work. After all, who would be a better authority? But I ran into snags regarding dates and important events that differed from book to book. Which source could I believe?

A biographer often plays detective, piecing together his or her subject's life. In Maria's case, problems with dates arose concerning the bank failure, the family's tours in Europe, and other matters pertaining to those turbulent years. To get the timing right, I closely compared Maria's books with one another. I also compared her description of personal events to world events, such as the rise of Hitler and the war that followed. It is possible that Maria simply forgot the exact order of events in the family's haste to leave Europe. To the best of my abilities, I have tried to correct any inconsistencies uncovered in Maria's own books.

It has been my intent to present Maria as the woman I perceive her to be—vibrant, bright, funny, wonderful. A woman whose life is as enchanting as any movie . . . and much more.

Chronology

1905   Maria Augusta Kutschera is born to Augusta and Karl Kutschera on January 26.

c.1907 Maria's mother dies.

1914   Maria's father dies.

1920   Maria graduates from high school.

1924   Maria graduates from teacher's college and enters Nonnberg Abbey.

1926   Maria comes to live with the Von Trapps.

1927   Maria marries Georg von Trapp.

1929   Rosmarie von Trapp is born.

1931   Eleonore von Trapp is born.

1936   The Von Trapps win the amateur contest at the Salzburg Music Festival.

1937   The Von Trapps perform at the Salzburg Music Festival and tour Europe.

1938   Germany takes over Austria. The Von Trapps flee Austria. The Von Trapps sail to the United States on the AMERICAN FARMER.

1939   Johannes von Trapp is born. The Von Trapps return to Europe. World War II begins on September 1. The Von Trapps return to the United States. F. C. Schang agrees to manage the Trapp Family Singers.

1942   The Von Trapps vacation in Stowe, Vermont, and Maria convinces Georg to buy a farmhouse.

1943   Werner and Rupert go off to war. The Von Trapps move to Stowe and begin building their home.

1944   Maria opens the first Trapp Family Music Camp.

1945   World War II ends on September 2.

1947   Maria and Georg set up the Austrian Relief Fund. Georg von Trapp dies. Maria miscarries her baby.

1948   Maria survives brain surgery. A new wing is added to the Von Trapp home, Cor Unum. Maria and her family become U.S. citizens and change their last names to Trapp.

1949   THE STORY OF THE TRAPP FAMILY SINGERS is published.

1950   The Trapp Family Singers tour South America and Europe.

1951   Martina dies.

1952   YESTERDAY, TODAY, AND FOREVER is published.

1955   The Trapp Family Singers tour Australia and New Zealand. They give their farewell concert at Town Hall in New York City.

1956   Maria travels to the South Seas with Father Wasner.

1959   A FAMILY ON WHEELS is published. Mary Martin visits Maria at Cor Unum. THE SOUND OF MUSIC opens on Broadway.

1965   THE SOUND OF MUSIC is released as a film.

1972   Hedwig dies in Austria. MARIA is published.

1987   Maria von Trapp dies on March 28.

Sources

Chapter 1

p. 8   Maria Augusta Trapp, *Maria: My Own Story* (Carol Stream, IL: Creation House, 1972), 14.

p. 14   Trapp, *Maria,* 19.

Chapter 2

p. 21   Trapp, *Maria,* 35.

p. 22   Trapp, *Maria,* 37.

p. 24   Trapp, *Maria,* 42.

Chapter 3

p. 29   Trapp, *Maria,* 54.

p. 30   Trapp, *Maria,* 54.

p. 36   Maria Augusta Trapp, *The Story of the Trapp Family Singers* (1949; reprint, Garden City, NY: Image Books, 1957), 49.

p. 38   Trapp, *Trapp Family Singers,* 57.

p. 38   Trapp, *Trapp Family Singers,* 58.

Chapter 4

p. 41   Trapp, *Maria,* 60.

p. 44   Trapp, *Trapp Family Singers,* 99.

p. 46   William Anderson, *The World of the Trapp Family* (Davison, MI: Anderson Publications, 1998), 39.

p. 46   Anderson, *The World of the Trapp Family,* 36.

p. 46   Trapp, *Maria,* 66.

Chapter 5

p. 53 Trapp, *Trapp Family Singers,* 128.
p. 54 Trapp, *Trapp Family Singers,* 129.
p. 55 Trapp, *Trapp Family Singers,* 134.
p. 56 Trapp, *Trapp Family Singers,* 140.

Chapter 6

p. 66 Trapp, *Trapp Family Singers,* 166.

Chapter 7

p. 68 Trapp, *Trapp Family Singers,* 178.
p. 71 Trapp, *Trapp Family Singers,* 183.
pp. 71–72 Trapp, *Trapp Family Singers,* 187.
p. 74 Trapp, *Trapp Family Singers,* 272–3.
p. 74 Maria Augusta Trapp, *A Family on Wheels: Further Adventures of the Trapp Family Singers* (Philadelphia: Lippincott, 1959), 44.
p. 75 Trapp, *Trapp Family Singers,* 201.

Chapter 8

p. 78 Trapp, *Trapp Family Singers,* 212.
p. 84 Trapp, *Trapp Family Singers,* 257.

Chapter 10

p. 96 Trapp, *Trapp Family Singers,* 150.

Bibliography

Anderson, William. *The World of the Trapp Family.* Davison, MI: Anderson Publications, 1998.

Trapp, Maria Augusta. *Around the Year with the Trapp Family.* New York: Pantheon, 1955.

Trapp, Maria Augusta. *A Family on Wheels: Further Adventures of the Trapp Family Singers.* Philadelphia: Lippincott, 1959.

Trapp, Maria Augusta. *Maria: My Own Story.* Carol Stream, IL: Creation House, 1972.

Trapp, Maria Augusta. *The Story of the Trapp Family Singers.* 1949. Reprint, Garden City, NY: Image Books, 1957.

Trapp, Maria Augusta. *Yesterday, Today, and Forever.* Philadelphia: Lippincott, 1952.

Index

Photos reproduced with permission from: © Trapp Family Archives, front cover (inset), pp. 2, 6 (all), 7 (top, bottom left, and middle), 8, 12 (both), 13, 18, 30 31, 33, 41, 44, 52, 59, 61, 74, 83, 87, 93, 103; © Robert Fried, front and back cover, pp. 2-3; © Photofest, back cover, p. 99; © UPI/Corbis-Bettman, pp. 7 (2nd, 3rd, 5th, 6th, and 7th on bottom from left), 70; © Hulton Getty Collection, pp. 20, 48, 49, 55, 65; © TRIP/M. Wilson, p. 23; © Gregor Schmid/Corbis, p. 26; AP Wide World Photos, p. 37; © David Brownell, p. 79; © Popperphoto/Archive Photos p. 45; Archive Photos, p. 80; © Billy Rose Collection, New York Public Library for the Performing Arts, p. 98; © Bettman/Corbis, pp. 21, 100.